I Get Wet

by Vicki Cobb

illustrated by Julia Gorton

■HarperCollins*Publishers*

For Benjamin Edward Trachtenberg
—V.C.

For the skateboarders and inline skaters
of Glen Ridge, New Jersey

—J.G.

The author gratefully acknowledges Dr. Myra Zarnowsky of Queens College for her help
in making this developmentally appropriate and Dr. Lee Tutt
of the Eastman Kodak Company for his technical expertise.
However, she takes full responsibility for the accuracy of the text.
She also extends a special thank-you to Andrea Curley for her brilliant editing.

I Get Wet
Text copyright © 2002 by Vicki Cobb
Illustrations copyright © 2002 by Julia Gorton
Manufactured in China. All rights reserved.
For information address HarperCollins Children's
Books, a division of HarperCollins Publishers,
10 East 53rd Street, New York, NY 10022.
www.harperchildrens.com

Library of Congress Cataloging-in-Publication Data
Cobb, Vicki.
I get wet / by Vicki Cobb ; illustrated
by Julia Gorton.
p.   cm.
ISBN 0-688-17838-3 — ISBN 0-688-17839-1 (lib. bdg.)
1. Water—Experiments—Juvenile literature.
[1. Water—Experiments. 2. Experiments.]
I. Gorton, Julia, ill. II. Title.
QC145.24 .C63 2002   00-049882
546'.22'078—dc21   CIP
                                        AC

Typography by Julia Gorton
09   10   11   12   13   SCP   10   9   8   7
First Edition

Note to the Reader

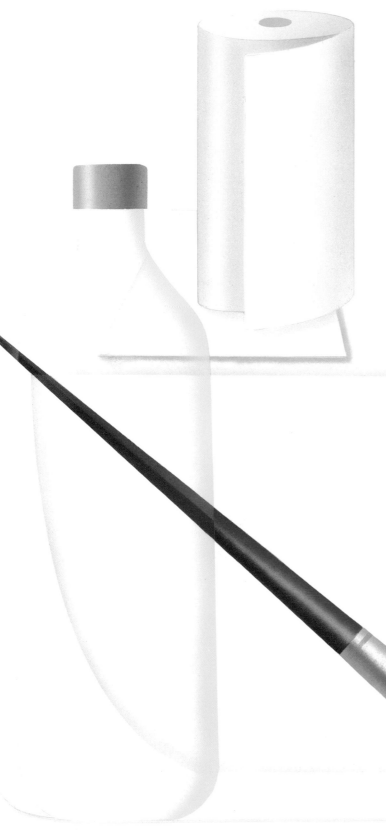

This book is designed so that your child can make discoveries. It poses a series of questions that can be answered by doing activities that temporarily take the child away from the book. The best way to use this book is to do the activities, without rushing, as they come up during your reading. Turn the page to the next part of the text only after the child has made the discovery. That way, the book will reinforce what the child has found out through experience.

Before you begin reading this book to your child, have on hand the following: several different containers, a paint-brush or a lock of hair, waxed paper, paper, and a paper towel. You will also need to be near a sink.

Know the fastest way to cool off on a hot summer day?

You get wet!

Know the easiest way to get clean?

Know what happens
when you stay out
in the rain?
You get wet! Water is
the stuff that wets you.
It is quite amazing.
You can see it. You can
feel it. But can you
answer this question?
What shape is water?

Here's how you can get your answer. Pour it into a glass. What shape is the water? Pour it from the glass into a bowl. Now what shape is the water? Pour it into other containers in your kitchen. What shape is the water?

Water is always the shape of the thing that's holding it. It is flat where it meets the air. If you pour water onto a flat surface, it spreads out. It follows itself as it goes down holes and into cracks. It flows. That's one reason why water can wet you. But it's not the only reason.

Water can flow because water sticks to itself.
Here's a way you can see water stick to itself.

Turn
on the
faucet.
Now turn it
almost all the
way off, but don't
tighten it. You
want water to
come out drop
by drop.

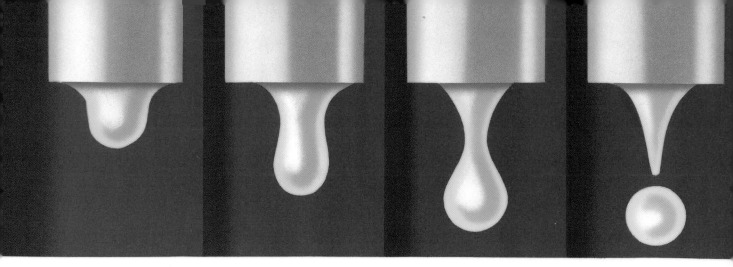

Watch as a drop of water comes out of the faucet.
First it forms a bulge.
It looks like a tiny bag of water.
Then the bulge gets longer and longer, stretching until
it breaks free and drops into the sink.
Perhaps that's why a drop of water is called a drop.

The surface of the water drop acts like a skin.
It is not a very strong skin.
When the drop of water gets heavy enough, the skin breaks.
If you could slow the drop down, you would see that skin pull
together and make the drop become

a
ball
as it
falls.

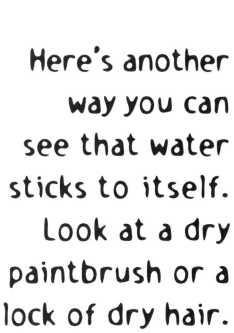

Here's another
way you can
see that water
sticks to itself.
Look at a dry
paintbrush or a
lock of dry hair.

The hairs don't stick together.

Now dip the paintbrush or the hair into some water and pull it out.

Ta da!

All the hairs are stuck together.

Water
wets you
because it can
flow. It flows
because it sticks
to itself even though
this stickiness is not very
strong. But there's still
another reason why
water can wet you.
Can you guess
what it is?

Do another experiment to find out.

Get a piece of waxed paper.

Put it under the faucet.

Take it out from under the faucet.

Touch it where the water was.

Is it wet?

Surprise!

The waxed paper is dry!

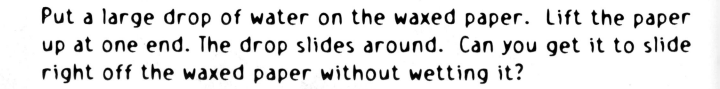

Put a large drop of water on the waxed paper. Lift the paper up at one end. The drop slides around. Can you get it to slide right off the waxed paper without wetting it?

You bet!

Water doesn't wet wax, or grease, or even a duck's back. A duck's feathers are coated with a kind of grease. That way ducks can stay dry after they dive under water.

Now put a drop of water on a piece of paper. What happens to the drop?

Cut a strip of
paper toweling.
Stick the end of
the paper towel
in a little bit
of water.

Watch what
happens to
the water.

Like magic the water moves up the paper.

The water wets paper because it sticks to the paper.

Water likes to stick to paper better than water likes to stick to itself. That's why the water travels up the paper toweling.

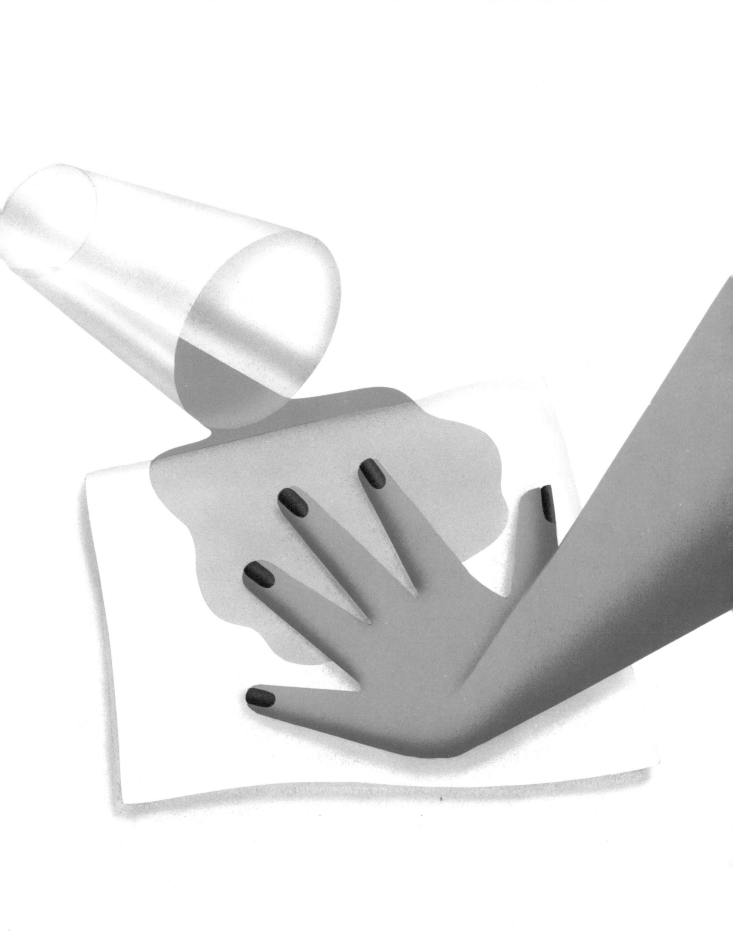

Does water

stick to you?

Put a drop

of water

on your hand.

Rub it around.

Water sticks

to you too.

Your skin also

soaks up water,

but not as fast

as paper soaks

up water.

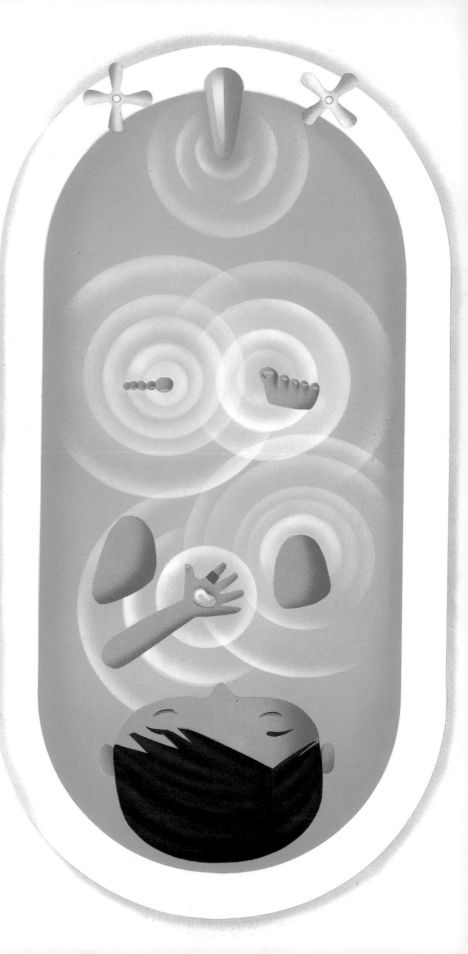

That's what makes
your fingers all wrinkled
when you've been soaking
in the tub awhile.

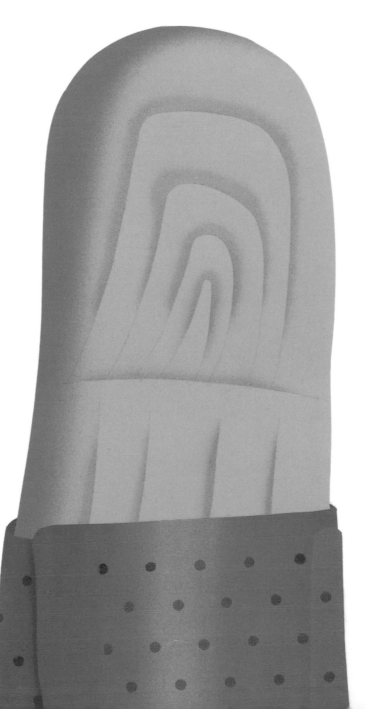

Water flows, it sticks to itself, and it sticks to you. That's why you get wet.